THE GARDEN OF FORGETTING

THE GARDEN OF FORGETTING

poems of love and loss

GWYNETH BARBER WOOD

PEEPAL TREE

First published in Great Britain in 2005
Peepal Tree Press Ltd
17 King's Avenue
Leeds LS6 1QS
UK

ISBN 1 84523 007 8

 Peepal Tree gratefully acknowledges Arts Council support

CONTENTS

VOICES FROM THE GARDEN OF FORGETTING

1

After rain, the earth mingling its spore
with the sun's heat reminds me of the suit
my father wore to those secret meetings
with the *brothers;* returning with mid-
night at his back and rum raising the ante
against a mirage that shifted with each bid
for the stained-glass front verandah door.

2

She left him the year the bougainvillea
forced its way through a crack in the wall
near the cellar. He didn't notice
their colour spreading like a bruise
nor a flagstone loosening like a rotting
tooth; he didn't notice until
the day no one scooped the soft-boiled
egg in a bowl at breakfast,
no one buttered his toast, and morning,
deprived of her cheerful discontent,
fell silent as an unanswered prayer.

3

Years on, like the prodigal returned,
he sought her, and for a while it seemed
we all were saved. But, like the warning
of a storm reversing, the wind turned back.
When his business failed we lost our home;
then everything changed. I'd see him hunched

at the edge of the bed, a sleepy shadow
impaled on the thorns of fallen dreams.
Then, one day, with the sweep of an epic
tale he left: the ash remains unclaimed.

4

That day, with the wind unyielding like the marble on
Miss P's headstone, I watched the tail-
lights of a car disappearing
inside morning and mist settling
as on a brooding moor in a classic novel.
Next thing I knew, the protagonist
was in some sleepy rural town
where box-kites combed the tops of mango
trees and the daughters of the soil
grew wild and stubborn, like guinea weed.

5

And then she came, an unheard thunder
followed by her voice, rain on zinc
like the chorus in a Greek tragedy,
and he was saved. Not by the black
beauty-mole on her raisin mouth
nor midnight hair wet with her salt,
but the tilt in her stillness:
someone who loved at last, without
conditions, who didn't nag about
'the sauce'. He put it down the day
his father died. Only then, they say,
did the voices in his head subside.

THE VERANDAH
(for WVB)

There is a place, distant in memory,
though nearer now than my own breath:
the time, a spring morning, the place, a verandah
where an unrepentant reveller, facing the unknown,
found at last the altar on which to lay her dreams.

The day was lyrical as the sea of heads on that street
in Port-au-Prince, near the Iron Market, and a boy whose eyes
never once met mine as he led me through a labyrinth
where pride watched from its sockets of sorrow.
I remember the pungent, musk-like odour of the wooden
sculptures, the baskets for all seasons: 'Buy this one
to keep your silver and gold trinkets, ma'mselle.'
'Look the paintings here!' *'Jolie comme vous, princesse!'*
A tap-tap, rainbowed, bursting at the seams, leaned left.

And as you gave it all a cursory glance,
I stood the ground of unknowing, focusing
on a distant range of hills, unyielding, unknowable,
the air tremulous as naivete,
and you, bespectacled, indifferent, behind your screen –
you who would one day define the horizon –
a gambler exchanging a cup of promise for a feast.

One day I wrote a tribute to you
and called it 'The Verandah' – not by any means
original, but then what is? Today, each time I roll
words half way up that hill,
I think of bamboo bent by the wind, and do not falter
as I write this, in your honour,
of the world I found on your verandah.

BLACK LOCUST

A door sealed shut, the plane rolls back, then forward
for the lift skyward, marking a chalk-white line
on the sky's cobalt, like the one separating
opposites on an inter-coastal highway.
Through a fog, a mountain like a woman full
with child heaves its belly toward night
even as the setting sun draws west.
Yet this poem is not about adversity
nor pathos, but triumph grappling with its brine.

I turn to that country where the dead are borne
to the hills and made there offerings for birds.
The bones return to Earth, leaving, they say, the soul to soar.
We're born, we die, and what stands between,
like children tumbling in the surf,
lives in the laughter and salt of forgetting
like the sky knowing both sides: the black
locust's upturned bloom withering
and the fledgling accidentally pushed from its nest.

What then should time recall: a wooden deck on water,
a face in clear sunlight, tiles on a carousel
conjuring words, or the hoarse breeze lifting its voice
so high not even God can hear it? Perhaps truth,
as the sea folds passion in a wave's white lace
or the soul's white eyes as we cross over.

Now, as day bends on familiar hills,
the sun's hot needle still draws its contradictions:
the sky bleeds rust on the black locust at evening
while morning consecrates its chaste-white flower.

VINCENT #1

This poem is not about the boy who grew
with the royal palms on Titchfield hill, who knew
the smell of fish gut lacing the salt breeze
as the boats stuttered ashore on dying waves.
It is not about a town that stirs gentility
with the treachery of an unknowable sea.

This poem is not about the man, a country
with its full moon in the centre of thinning grey
rising like a hedge over a narrow margin
and eyes that looked out on their happy grief;
nor earth, as he dragged his feet
to the place he'd come to know,
as chains shuffle their sorrow.

Behind the market, a woman stabs at ice
as if it were the man she'd left asleep with the stale
night on his breath. The scales splatter her face.
'You want any fresh snapper today?' A soprano tilts
in the breeze, then flattens, like the eyes for sale.

No, this poem is not about you, Vincent,
for I disliked you without reason, and that was all.
Perhaps, it was insidious as the scent
of your cologne unsettling the solitude, a call
from the garden where conditions grew.
I tried to ignore you but you muttered like the river
riding hot stones on that day in red July.

This poem is about her, ashes stored in an urn,
a purple fish in a bowl that dances when I sing,
the garden of love she watered with conditions,
bitter lees left in a cup,
drawers splayed like someone's obsession,
and humility – the sea that suffered me up.

VINCENT # 2

Unafraid of ghosts, you've worn time's scales
like slaves their callused soles, while mine
latched in the rhyme of measured tiers
weep soundlessly between the lines.

Looking back, I see you, patient as need
in pride's bald face, your sorrow resounding
like the flightless picking at pulp-less seed,
a season's burden seeping on sacred ground.

At night, the shutters closing on some rural lore
where spirits drag their chains, the terra cotta bowl
I found among the webbed silks of a spider's store,
holds back her ash, all that remains.

And still the sun due east, even as Anancy's wry
laughter catches like hair in bramble, the lump
in grief's throat hardens, like the candle's eyeless
tears, or as a forest's blackened stumps

drizzles ash on blind tomorrow. You never knew,
Vincent, like you I married the sun and since rise as
he rises. Here at my screen, the solitary knocking at dew,
I rewrite the chordless lines until the chorus rises.

INFINITY

(for my son)

Four o'clock and wide-awake –
Autumnal chill seeps through the crack
above my narrow bed. A sky like slate.

It seems like yesterday cicadas trilled
their defiant chatter to the wind
as someone's bashment in the valley welled

up into my head. But now I only hear
the silence of a city street, the luminescent tick,
and you, a wall away.

I remember the day you asked
how much I loved you.
Like the sky, I said, as wide as the sky…
"I love you to 'finity", you said; you were three.

Twenty years on, we passed a silver birch
spilling its sorrow on the earth
at the place where the old stone church still stands

near a busy London street, and I am grateful for that sky
as I have been innumerable times since then,
even as I grappled with loss the year

you disappeared leaving only the memory,
like the pain reflected in stained glass,
where innocence promised infinity.

EASTER

(For Sean)

The season of mourning come again, its dry
wind unsettles branches brittle as the frail
stalks of gungo outside my window, and the loaf-
brown pods hanging from withered stems. I cry
for birds too long in the nest, for torn wings
that failed at flight, and scorn remorse's impotence.

Can the wing wrest from the jaws of pain
as a rainbow arcs through rain? And will the dark-
ness ever leave? Know only there is God, although the vain
calling of His name will not free the trembling heart
or roll the stone from a cave's mouth.

The years pass, the dreams die, and then there's death.
The soul's tired footfalls echo soundlessly
as twilight dusting violets near a hedge,
or night, the inflamed sun with its blear breath.
Then yearning, bittersweet as the thorn of lust,
stemmed to bursting, loses its edge.

FATHER

Father, I thought I'd find you in
the sun's conflagrations – sometimes
I'd hear your voice in a howling wind.
Last night in the starlit sky I saw
a meteor as it arc'd to earth,
leaving nothing in its wake
but a ghost-white trail and a pale moon.

Father, I've looked for you in every face;
one day I felt the sun around my waist –
no one ever held my life in that way,
whatever that means – you weren't perfect, either –
always, they were too weak, too strong, too
human, never wrong… all but one.
Every morning now I watch him dress, like you,
from the merino vest to the white 'kerchief,
the spit-shine black lace-up shoes. Is you
sen' him to haunt me? So many questions,
hanging like black apostrophes in the wind.

One day, perhaps, I'll find you in a sweep
of lilac, where it seeps through the dusk-dark leaves
of the poor man's orchid – you know the one.
It started as a dry stalk, but now the blossoms
lie around my feet like fallen dreams.

These days, when I remember you, a mist
passes across my eyes like a drizzle through
a bright rainbow, as it blesses the valley below.
In the night sky I look for you in Mars,
but find you instead in a fallen star.

THE FAN PALM

I sat on the steps of the old great house while water
poured off the roof, down a guttering rain-spout,
sucking on a cigarette and watching its zeros rise
then dissipate like vapour on hot asphalt. A fan palm

swayed in the wind – it reminded me
of the dog nodding in the back of the Austin taxicab
on the days my father trailed Aunt Lara
after picking me up from school.

I can see her through a rear window wiping
the warm beads from the powdered provinces of her age.
At a crossroads, as if unsure, the car inched along,
then indicated: a lizard flicking an amber warning.

Twenty years before, she was powerful as the breeze
that stifled me when I walked with my mother at the sea's edge,
her hem trailing in the splash, and ripe almond leaves
squelching under her feet.

What was it about Lara –
reticence wrapped in the hum of an old love song? –
that my father loved her? The year he died,
no one asked about her, nor saw the light in her window

flicker, then go out. At the end, what is truth,
the fan palm losing its colour at day's closing,
the ground bearing the load of autumn's lust,
or the wounded leaving their mark on Earth?

I stub out my cigarette and watch a humming-
bird fly backwards from a flower as if
recoiling from the pain of its beauty or its own
as silent as the sorrow looking on.

AUTUMN

This morning I watch him make his way
down the narrow brick path into the pale
sunlight, the way he's done for the past
five years. Look how he turns back for the last
goodbye, the way he always does. I wait
until he throws the morning paper
and catch it hurtling through the air — then stay
to watch the butterflies chase each other around
the red hibiscus beyond the gate.

I envy them their world of flight and mirth,
how lithely their wings flutter! How lightly they
anoint the flowers hanging closest to the earth!

The days get shorter after fifty and
endurance wanes. But nothing else changes:
love is the same, and autumn, if anything, wears
its passion-colour more considerately than spring,
for it has known branches heavy with summer
and the dank brown of the sated earth.

So, when the shadow of this dying day creases
the backs of the hills outside my window, I shall watch
while evening draws the marrow from the sun.
With dawn, perhaps, a straightened joy will come —
the rectitude that resolution faces —
and, like these butterflies in the flowers' grasp,
lap at the memories, until time ceases.

SUNDAY MORNING

Sunday morning, and beyond the glass the trees
seem stencilled on the white page.

I have missed the rooster calling through the haze;
that unrelenting voice from dawn's white surge,

even as the amnesiac lamp at the corner shop
flickers where early risers double back for home.

It used to be the village church bells ringing, or a ship's
bellow as it inched into a seaside town;

now voices wake me up and draw me to this place.
I wait for him or her, whoever comes: the muse

that seasons my thin broth, a wooden spoon
turned faceless as the sorrow only hermits choose.

It wasn't always like that: once Sunday meant sleep-ins
and slow awakenings from dreams. But now I rise

and copy out the lines that they lay bare,
their meaning scanned by sleep, before time's weakening sighs.

In an ideal world, God is the word,
and the word is God. How everything has changed!

Now, the only sparks on startled faces are the tears
where the shadowless roam unheard.

The earth is wet: the night-sky's conflagration isn't stars.

REFLECTION

Just when you think
you have all the answers,
that you're not afraid any more,
it comes:
the unheard thunder,
the lightning flight of arrows,
then the pain –
the pain that slackens
but is always there
with everything you do,
that rises from the dark
of your own neglect,
the tears that come
with first light,
in spite of loved ones, in spite of loving.
In the face of your sorrow
the white cat blinks and turns away.
The dew gleams on the grass.

BLACK TUESDAY

Over the world a black sky frowns
while time stares deadpan from a bedside table.

What help for grief when terror's thorn
lets the fruit of our striving dry on the sable

earth. At morning, while the light hardens
on roofs where sorrow made its bed,

I recall a green chair in a back garden
between the potted geranium and an abandoned shed.

Three trains have brought me back to the place
I now call second home; I found the key

under the grey bin by the front door and woodlice
scuttling black into the yellow day.

I turn the lock and climb the stairs to a room
no bigger than a crypt for a king and queen;

twisted metal glints like gold as I dream
in vain; the shottas sneer as they force a home.

Tomorrow, will twilight comb September's leaves
or an empty sky where death mushrooms above

that purple hour? I remember terror's eyes, like scales,
and that time when eyes hid nothing, not even the pain of love.

In this silence, where inner voices mumble at a sky-
line now erased, a window remains slack

with disbelief, the universe's hollow why.
A black beast is circling at our backs.

THE ABYSS

Today like any other day the sun will rise
and set its yellow yolk on the Hudson River

even as death's thin layer clouds the eyes
of grief like cataracts, reflection's faceless mirror.

Elsewhere, the sky's red gauze is not a desert
night, no tracts of powdery white, no stars,

only blank stares where the chadors lie inert
on cracked earth, and the dry gutters of tears.

How can hatred leaking from a darkening sky
fathom a nation where unseeing eyes roll back,

their white couching the stain of war! At the end, we lie
as one, implicit, as Islam's prostrate flock.

And now the boundless earth: no chalk-white line
separates the poles. The silence insists, like the buzz

of flies on the dead, as mornings choked with pain
find still smoking craters where once life was.

COURAGE – AFTER THE 6.00 PM NEWS
(for Mrs Gayle)

Today as I headed for the hills
between the waxen glare
of the sun on snaking cars and a poet tailing
a poem's salt-sheet to an audio tape,
as if to numb the sorrow weeping
under passion's layers, like a head
thrown back in ecstasy as a maestro
works the scales in black and ivory,
the sweet anguish of a sad strain
unsettling a mellow wind,
I heard a woman, new-widowed
after 40 years, say:

'I will not leave this home, the grave-
yard of a dream.'
Of her, like the old
salt fighting adversity,
I think what courage grows from grief.

SUZI V.

In the dark waters
the sun finds her,
a land breeze stirring.

Once a proud beauty
leaning in the wind,
now she's becalmed

like the sun's red yolk
streaming across
an azure sky,

like grief rising
in passion's throat
as the wind dies –

while out in the wider
sea, a sleek 'cat'
shines like memory,

purling to windward
in long zeds
disappearing

into the night.

SORROW'S EVE

From the neighbouring yard a scythe levelling grass
is the only sound this Christmas eve.
No smell of pine, nor ham's clove-pinched fat
nor poncha crème with its induced white heat
suffuses these thin walls as memory recedes.

The scentless night wears yellow, black and green,
the darkened street looks back through lit white lashes.
Their fruitless gardens bloom goblins and gnomes.
The reindeer are silent as the absent snow.

And yet a cup is full, even as the embattled heart
remains undone by time's remembered love:
the pungent smell of fruit-soaked wine,
an apron gathering that season's gungo peas,
coffee bubbling on the Caledonia stove,
our laughter prickling the cool September breeze,
and then, before the silence, fear's tuneless whistle...

And still a question's hook hangs in the air:
whichever fork in the road we choose, is there not death?
Yet, while its hiss flickers like a tongue at the tree of life,
I remember him, featureless as the platform backed away,
leaving white December covering the earth.

OLD STRAINS

One Sunday morning the Boulevard changed beat:
no exhaust fumes choking the busy street,
nor snaking lines inching past proffered wipers –
only the smell of jerk spiked with pimento and
craft vendors parked inside their stalls
and the hoarse rumble of black bass speakers.

I walked slowly, looking for familiar signs.
Nothing caught my eye except the man I'd married –
he never saw me till the bass lowered the boom,
and the sky widened – "Hi honey, are you hungry?"
began and ended our tour with metaphor.

In our suburban quiet, dusk
blotted the day's heat, blurring the lines
that had me braced against the warp of history,
and sadness leaked in dying strains
where the years tiptoed through memory,
softening the footfalls of a changing guard,

While outside, the scented night-blooming cereus
exploded its flowers, like a sky of stars.

THE TRIAL

'He loved me once, my lord, that is true,
but coming and going the seasons tapered that lure,
until the sun set on indifference.
If I'd let the beast live, he would no doubt
have torn flowers from their innocence,
while autumn's unplucked fruit, ripened to bursting,
would fall, becoming mulch.
And that, my lord, is why I had
to intervene, in the name of destiny.
And that, ladies and gentlemen, is all –
the still, sad voice of unrequited love.'

Seven years after they first met, she recalled
their walks by the midnight sea – had he forgotten,
or had she imagined the grievous joy, the happy tears?
He'd come to her that night, an injured bird
asking for death – to die in her love.
She gave him her gift, his shuddering fall.
Exhibit A in the courtroom pled silence.
And in the unresolved fog of such misery,
the jury hung. Her sentence was
to go on living, and that was all –
the still, sad voice of unrequited love.

THE BLANK SCREEN

One morning I awoke and felt the room
spinning round the earth; daylight streamed
through the window and a wave of sick mirth
washed over me as I recalled the debt
I owed to God. Might as well be dead.
Too early for breakfast, too late for regret,
I switched on the screen instead.

I had chosen the lonely road, the dark
of poetry, but that faithless bitch, the muse,
was nowhere to be found. The stark
screen stared back at me. The clock stuck six.
Time for my cigarette and caffeine fix.
Nothing had changed. I'd be here till sunset.

The morning stretched like eternity,
I thought of the heaven I'd never know.
Things might have been different but for the slow
roil of temptation that drew me from
contentment's pond into the maelstrom.

When the moon slips from the mountain's grasp,
she may break her silence.
Then I'll be free from these imprisoning lines,
and this blank screen.

THE WRETCHED

Are they who mutter
at cars snaking on busy streets at rush hour,
or the stitched smiles of privilege
looking back through a tinted pane;

who, from a washed verandah, gaze
absently beyond the chain-linked dawn,
like patrol boats guarding foreign water;

who live in darkness like the oil-
birds in the South, responding only
to the sonic click bouncing from a cave wall,

who are never certain which street
becomes a cul-de-sac, or how a tongue,
engaged, can trigger death's cool sleep.

By design, or accident, we are all
casualties of struggle; evolving from
dark through darkness only to return,

our echoes left hanging like love's white heat
beneath the smouldering ash of grey December.

THE YUCCA

I

The white yucca blossom mounts on a stem of thorns,
a place only the fortunate can attest to knowing.
You'll know you've been there if you can hear the song
of the wood slaves scratching their throat at evening
or mist settling like a spine down a valley;
for passion moves through unexpected channels.

II

There the breeze lifts its hoarse voice a cappella,
the earth pimento, where the hearth is a dutchie;
but here the tears of morning tremble on sharp blades
for grief, like unrequited love, never sleeps
and the mouths of rivers crust white like hunger.

III

Once worth was measured with a laurel wreath
while yearning fellowed sleep to taste the wine
or languished in the cell of a thousand words:
'Winter does not go without looking backward',
Yet, like cows chewing north, the sorrow numbs
with a Q of rum; then domino is king.

IV

The seasons call to mind learned memory
perhaps, the idea of order, that part of history
stitched tight like hurt, when, unresolved, passion weeps.
What stays is pain, persistent as bamboo in the wind.
Therefore, whatever dawn lights up the sky, I sing.

OLD AGE

August's ripe leaves steal past a window
as an island autumn turns unseen.
How certainly all beauty fades, except
perhaps the soul's — I switch the screen.

Even as I write these words for you, they may
disintegrate like a kaleidoscope's glass pieces;
yet I recall when once they grew
between the dream and empty spaces.

You suffered youth like the long days ripening
on a kitchen table the passion fruit's wax stare
in the cobalt ceramic bowl; not like the fir reciting
its evergreen ode to your season's silver hair.

Yet like sorrow, the heart denied, you are the face
I shall expect to see as rage quiets, as in sleep,
and a slowing wave spreads its white spume at your feet,
or morning, the promise it can never keep.

BRISTOL BOY

(in memory of Richard Barber)

Through a crack in the great oak door, beside the sacred heart,
the Blessed Virgin cradles the infant Jesus in her arms:
On a morning in pale April, fifty something years ago,
with crocuses pushing through the baptized earth,
the Avon straining at the banks, and boats
inching through its gorge, a child was born –
not the messiah, but the only son of a doctor
in a grey, southwestern seaport town.

Years on, paternal illness saw them on the coast, near Durban,
where long walks on the beach with his trusted retriever
bronzed his skin like the gilded cherub that graced the top
of the Christmas tree the year Aunt Rose crossed over.
One day, a dream of the islands found him on a banana
boat, in the grimace of the brackish Atlantic, each knot
binding him nearer to the peacock blues and greens
fanning the conflicting currents of the Caribbean.

He chose one for her enigmatic peaks and a Mona Lisa
smile framed by velvet furrows, and there he spawned
a seed in the shadow of the flame tree planted near
the wall, the one Taby built on Sundays stone by stone,
his toothless smile like the moon riding dark scallops.
Old faithful, he'd still be there, curved like a bow,
when he returned from worshipping the briny god,
the spinnaker flapping as he tacked the flattening sea.

One Christmas, that season's gungo peas heavy on their branches
and an icy wind rattling the flame pods like shak-shak,
with night deepening the indigo shawl of the Blue Mountains
and the Hope river shushing past the window where she dreamed,

a sound like a sling-shot dropping a white wing in sultry August,
like a wood-slave plopping on the cedar floor in another life,
and with the city looking on, a stain lengthened on concrete.

Now, as the Avon settles at low tide, you may hear the sea gulls' throaty
cries as they circle a ketch stuck in the muddy silt.
All bear the mark of passion's sorrow.

SPRING

I dreamt of Paris in the spring
and how it might have been: hearing you sing
in the shower, and the smell of coffee brewing
in a corner of some cheap *pension,* smoking
Gauloises, the ashtray brimming and the pale
April gleam fanning its yellow tail
through blinds at the day's awakening – and silence
hanging on the sill of still-sleepy conscience.
Then, awkwardly, we'd rise and watch the rain
snake along the glistening margins of our pain,
and I'd smell the rotting leaves, and you'd ask the time,
and then recall some rendezvous at nine.
How lives become wastelands! But then,
who gives a damn but God that daylight finds
two thieves recoiling from the sun's blank gaze?
When the summer's gone, why count the days?

THE BRINE OF LOSS

If you leave before the end of day,
while time's wounds weep beneath the skin,
my wish would be, each morning you awaken,
your east will be what you were to me
when I loved you.

If you go before morning drains the night
with shadow still deepening the hills,
I'd only mourn the words I didn't say:
you were the best I'd ever been.

As the mountain wears the char of flames
that once licked at its throat,
I have given you the crown you wear.
The questions that were never asked;
their answers lie in the trail of scattered bones.

I have looked far enough into the dark of love;
the songs I once sung ring with a hollow chime;
the sorrow of a squandered life is such a grievous thing
that I would sip the brine of loss: proof I have lived.

THAT SUMMER

I remember, that summer, the salt air
crept under my skin and stayed there.
the days seemed endless as we lay
in the dream-shade, turning the world away.

That summer the jasmine seemed more
pungent than the year before,
the rough wet wind of autumn, colder.
Then, as the year grew older

the sorrow of our dark unknowing
turned stark as winter branches in
an icy wind, and our souls knew grief
in the silence of a fluttering leaf.

Now in the quiet of memory,
as evening inflames the hills
at the end of a day in red July,
I remember you, that summer, still.

SMITH'S COVE

I

I remembered one sky from the bluff of a quiet cove
as I lay looking up through scorched almond leaves,
the waves welling and spilling their secrets in
the honeycomb, the salt spray blurring your words.

II

At the heart of any storm silence bleeds
like passion separating from its sentence, black
spines deepening the hills as day withdraws,
when for a while, it seems, sorrow recedes.

III

Morning's slate sky, night shedding its scales,
interring the brine of losing you not even loving
can erase, that stays in spite of all,
and the dog whimpering at the hint of rain.

PARADISE'S PARADOX
(for VCCA)

Where the sea's slow hand peels back the sorrow,
I write these words on an island breeze:
of your quiet shelter, thirst and hunger,
slacking in yellow as tomorrow
drowns in yesterday's dream.

At the heart of wilderness the signs obscure.
How to know the way when the path forks?
Between the tines of hesitation things become,
then it is the sacrifice that threads to our door.

Paradoxes: the dignity
of indigo under a cool sun,
of a cardinal wearing the tree's sleeveless arm,
and, in long grass, black snakes sliding
in the jasmine-sweetened air.

Now, away from your mooring, in a silence,
like keels slicing blue water, a ketch is loose,
the wind at her heel. In her wake, salt stains on truth
and the sun's searing indifference.

THE ARTIST

He sits at the edge of the sun-bleached pier, the wind
turning the leaves of an open book near him,
his heart mirroring the cumulus clouds
masking the last of a cobalt sky.
On rainy afternoons he'd sketch her,
as she lay dreamless, twirling her tangled hair:
her milk-white breast pouting from the curve of her arm.
Was it her absent smile that snared him then?
What was the desert in her sighs?
Between her upturned nose and the quiver in
her chin, the answers sting his weary eyes
like a salty rain. Only a desperate love could lure
him back to the well within her thighs.
The sea is calm. Her damp silk dries.

CAT

Waking from dreams, I see him
on the window ledge,
contemplating the brilliant green

hummingbird hovering near.
His jaw slackens
as he watches it, calculating the one deft
movement that would tear

the beating heart from its solitude.
Then, silent as a broken wing's
involuntary flutter ceasing,

indifference blinks and walks away,
leaving the morning wet
as the black earth after rain.

REMEMBERING THIRA

(for Jan)

Often I'd reflect on how the light
affected the houses on Thira
where we met once: the sun gleaming white
on whitewashed walls against the crisp
clean blue of the Mediterranean sky;
not like the eyes mirroring the black
shadows of birds flowing by,
their wings' sprawling consonants…

The nights are cold there in September,
and the birds migrate to warmer climes.
Only the white light, the old and the curious stay behind.

The clock chimed midnight as we left the taverna
where men from the village danced together,
and made our way through narrow streets
toward the old church, to the crossroads where we lived.
Sometimes, like goats chewing at a hedge,
we'd stop to savour the last of midnight
like darkness at its edge, or like the hour
when clarity shifts its focus, and lilac coarsens the air.
Now I look back and find her weeping
at a map, the one that traced Alexander's trek
from Macedonia to Babylon and death:
fervour imagining loss, or a former life.

The old Greek freighter pushed out of port,
leaning its grey unfathomable weight,
belching thick black smoke. Some miles out,
the greasy deck-hand plugging a leak
with an old rag reminded me
of a derelict carrying his life in a paper bag.
I looked out at the dark ocean kicking up froth

at the edge of a wave, then turned back to the cloth
stemming its salt tears.

After the Acropolis, I never saw her again,
until a dream of Minshall's 'River' –
a mask streaked white, years lost in the shallows –
And memory leapt like nymphets across a stage,
their white streaming bright colour!
From that day, I knew I couldn't lose her.

In the 'River', I found the riches of Thira,
her smile in its reflection and a heart fluttering
like a single leaf slowly, slowly, falling.

THE COVENANT
(for Rudi)

So the past is past – he's been ordained
and dwells within his solemn austerity:
black hat and robe, his bliss a narrow bed
and a Tilly lamp flickering its orange glow
from the bald surface of a bedside table.
Through a window, a brighter day infuses him
but the sky now is a torpid grey, and in
the dark of coming age he's locked inside
the sacred promise of eternity.

I remember a time in ripening years
when we lay on the sand, water lapping our sentences,
the sun framing our dreams in brilliance, while he
combed the sea for spiny urchins, and fed me
their exotic roe, and watched my nose wrinkle,
his eyes crinkling with the sky's reflection.

Years on I went back there to find the land
in drought-torn contradiction: one weathered fir
amid the spring of greens, and wind
tussling the ripe almond leaves on brittle branches.

The waves were dying
on the reef, making ripples in the bay,
the setting sun gave way to a quarter moon
and a sky sprinkled with stars,
and in the quiet trove of memory
I bathed deep thought in the gleam of galaxies.

But man is no more free from original sin
than the shore from the sea's insistent spill,
or the sky from the whip-ray's shadow as it stalks
the dark waters of Poseidon's cradle –
Or my friend from his solemn isolation,
or me, behind the bars of this ever deepening silence.

A DAY AT SAN PIPER

Bright sky, the house at the water's edge, the blonde
in the red and white one-piece now centre stage,
the crowd hanging on every word, the breeze
carrying their laughter; on its tail, her pain.

It was the first time I noticed the swelling tide,
the sea lapping at the lip of the wooden deck
as the man arced into the water, while I
pushed off toward an island across the bay.

Occasionally he'd glance behind, unlike swans gliding
on a lake's glass face, that never look back,
as if reconciled the journey ends in death.
Landed at leeward we begin the climb – like that.

At the top, a bench cut from a bamboo grove
looks out beyond a tree's torn arm,
'How many birds?' 'Only the one.'
'Whitecaps!' We laugh at blindness. Nothing has changed

though change has come; the years have borne their fruit.
Her words kept haunting me: 'I still can't come to terms
with the mirror's face. That woman seems much sterner now!'
I looked out on the bay where a piper churned the waves
and wondered whether that face had once known vain pursuit.

A LIGHT LEFT ON
(for Dayton)

Sometimes in your eyes I see him lingering,
dark, strikingly handsome… and your longing,
especially on those long, starless evenings
when conversations with the brothers become a road
disappearing into the dark,
when their images waver to a blur, and you see him
and imagine how it might have been
if the sea had rejected him that day.

Years later, when she followed him,
your sisters took her place; and now I see
the face of a man whose kindness never looks away.

For you, now father of your own,
see in your son's eyes bewilderment
as he reluctantly stretches from your sight.
And she is right behind him, the years
ripening her laughter to black velvet.
Then, one day, you surrender her
to the way of another man.

These children of another generation,
baptized in a father's sorrow,
have known the deafening chorus of cicadas,
the heavy-scented night jasmine,
and your aftershave as you kissed them
and left the room, leaving a light on.

OLD FRIEND

I saw a friend the other day;
she looked the same, but for the sky
like a whitened ash mirroring the passion lost
to her watchful eye. And yet the wicks
of her mouth still curled the way they did
when she beguiled the world!
Now as we sift the dreams of yesterday
I watch the sun erase the August sky
as her familiar shadow becomes small
and take my cup of sorrow as it comes.

TIME

On such a day, where the dry wind scatters promise,
we thrash like the sea under the rain,

the remembered life flitting eyeless
as memory recalls the piper's haunting strain.

Fifty, the age some grapple with eternity –
What then of years before, when we, like vines,

spring from the earth to curl soft tendrils on a tree,
or like the fir needling seasons with green thorns.

I have watched an old friend sip her cup of fate,
even as you walk her through the maize of yesterday.

Now, in your narrowing pew, she awaits
release from the sun's white gaze. Some say,

it is you who rock our infants while they sleep,
tolerate unsteady feet, then puberty's glass stare;

punctuate black holes with stars, even we weep,
our footfalls echoing soundlessly, like years.

Often, by a quiet bay where I watch the powdery sand
dissolve as waves drag back the sea's course grains:

I wonder, when the pitch flattens, what hand
will stay our fear while Neptune's grave still churns.

FOR AULD LANG SYNE
(for BB)

That was how I remember her, slender
as a reed and berry-brown, with her deer-like eyes
that darted when she spoke. There began
the stalk of a friendship that would root
as deep as silence and
near as mist settling on the morning.

I have longed for those green years
that changed our lives – for better or worse,
I'm never sure. Now, when I strip
the layers away, poignancy leaks
from the wound, and the mirror blurs...
One day I learnt
the blossoms of the poui spiral backward
toward the earth, never losing the sky...

Morning was a jeep rattling
round a thirsty mountain road, until we reached
the garden where forgetting grew,
and walked between the lines of statis
and crimson coffee berries, burnished by the sun –
we picked one or two
and sucked the sweet pulp from the bitter bean,
wiping the stain from memory –
until the day fell silent on the western hills
and cast a lemon glare on the scattered shards
of porcelain on the path, and on the yellow
bamboo groves sentinelling the black slopes.
We talked of quiet bays and why fate chose
for some the stormy sea, and had no regrets;
we sipped the wine
and drained the lees
for Auld Lang Syne.

Someday there'll be a tribute to her hair,
and how she lost it all, and found her soul
in the tumour of a dark and desperate time,
her humour steeled against that bitter sea.
You may find her in the spiny ferns,
in the hoarse wind rattling the sheaves
of sugarcane on a drought-torn summer's day,
or at her favourite haunt, with bedtime near:
her feet dangling at the water's edge as dusk-
ripened silhouettes tiptoe across the bay.

The world's unfair, and then we die,
but courage only rises in the throat of grief –
as when the wounded deer one last time stands
on the shadowy outline of a hill,
its signature against the sky.

THE DANCER
(for Clive T.)

Like a dancer poised *en l'air*,
a pandanus' shadow lengthens;
the suspended tendrils arch earthward.
Inside his mind-kaleidoscope water prickles
the sculpted lion's unseeing eye
then plummets to a swirling underworld.
There, no devilfish shadows move.
An angel fish undulates her reedlike languor;
the lucent fins curl, extend, gossamer,
until, like a storm reversing,
intemperance pirouettes in the eye.
Outside, the mynahs chatter from their perches;
the dancer waits.
The hoarse theme crescendos, unlocks a cloud,
and a bursting heart soars skyward.

MAGNOLIA
(for WGS)

I climb the stairs of the old great house where she used to live
and stand at the window of a decade or more. There, in the shade
of the magnolia, I see her plain as the spring breeze stirring
the snowy blossoms on bare branches. And I recalled St. Marco's square
the day they met and the white, white pigeons circling midnight hair,
but that was long ago. Now dusk-green leaves dapple yellow August
and the light on the cotton sheets where they'd made their bed,
white framing fawn-brown skin and eyes, black like ackee-seeds.

You have seen her in the painting of sorrow's smile,
the vacant stares in an old Spanish village by the sea
where women in black sit out on the sidewalk, waiting for eternity.
She was the waif you saw scurrying in front of the cathedral
on Easter morning, her eyes downcast, under a black mantilla;
dropping Easter Lilies on the freshly washed piazza
as she stopped to make the sign of the cross.
She'd loved with the joy and sadness of a perfect circle.

Now she gazes absently across the morning,
while the other woman wears her gift of sadness
like a village hoping seaward for their missing men,
and towns are inconsolable as birds swarm south.

WHITE GARDENIA
(for Rachel)

The flowers marched in lockstep with
her father's love of symmetry.
He'd spend long hours amid their colours
alone, returning at noon, his fair skin roasted
like Sunday morning's grind of coffee beans
bubbling on the back burner of a country stove.

She'd see him coming, straw-hatted, arms akimbo:
an old clay pot brimming with treasure
from the soil; and her eyes would follow, she, his shadow,
longing for some sign, whim or pleasure,
till he, revelling, obliged:
A special errand. 'Suck-up', they called her:
two sisters recounting memories.

One day I asked her what Nyumbani meant.
Clouds dotted the sky's blue basin,
archipelagal, white, quiescent,
as if waiting to ascribe the moment
that day would draw the line.
"Swahili, for peace in my home."
She exhaled the gardenia-scented air.

Like peaks hunched in their watch from year to year,
the spirits of the departed hover near,
like the shrine of a lost life locked in stone.
In red July with a truck towing
cyclists too weary to climb the dusty mountain road,
she retreats for shelter to an English town.

THE SOLSTICE MOON
(for SJ)

She'd often bring some thoughtful treasure,
once, flowers from the countryside
pressed in a silver brooch;
but even their beauty could not measure
her joy in giving, or the sadness in her eyes.

One day she brought a stone from some Atlantic shore;
as if still fresh spewed by the sea it bore
the damp scent of memory,
finely wound with silver strands,
translucent in the gleam of her faint lamp.

These days when waves crash on her shore,
I bring small treasures of my own;
never question the salt-trails on her cheeks,
or what had gone before,
but find her in the quiet crackle of the phone.

Now when the night winds rail and rattle
the woman tongue, it's always her
laughter I remember;
for through the dark days and endless prattle
we knew the solstice moon would not defer
its brilliance that December.

JERUSALEM THORN
(for BB)

I remember the days slowing as black October tightened
its low ceiling. We'd watch the birds like statues on
the Coolie plum fly off in chalk-white lanes, frightened
perhaps by the dark circling as footfalls hurried on.

Those Fridays, like religion, the faithful came.
Choir practice, she'd say, the sacramental wine
awakening what joy there was beneath the pain.
The times alone, the trees provided grist for poems:

I had not seen the Jerusalem thorn's gold bloom and yet
its promise was sufficient in a name –
a city elevated between two seas, dry summer heat,
winter's reluctant theme, and a sea's dead foam.

But this is not about the Holy City where the light
reflects the pinkish-white of buildings, the Wall's
sorrow, nor betrayal's remorse as He awaited
the hour, the dark of Gethsemane growing pale.

This is about the street where friends grew up, the right
of choice, knowing how to go when the road narrows,
how to march sideways from the dwindling night
like soldier crabs, how to watch the spent arrow

without regret. Still, the rain marries earth with its bright
band arcing across renewal, and hope's pale glimmer
remains the seed of love, even as we lose sight
of the promise sleeping in the infolded flower.

LETTER

(for Dayton)

At dawn the distant ranges pencil
their indigo line on the sky's clean sill,
and in the silence, like hair turning white,
absence exacts its bleak measure.

Beloved, I have missed you as never before.
I wake to light seeping under the door
and think you a wall away, running cool water
on a 4:00 a.m. migraine (how impotent the lover

to assuage pain!). Asleep, I saw your face
where the river of your Arawak inheritance,
pulsing, has left no ravage of the years –
not like this mirror chipping in layers.

I speak my truth as the cobalt Aegean,
expressing its salt, keeps the memory keen.
Like a prodigal remembering the once-spurned fold,
I yearn for you and my thirst to be reconciled.

Hardship leaks as we brace against the rain
like opposites pulling on vain strands of hope.
A fickle wind can blow any ketch off course.
The dream, a masked rider on a black horse

galloping toward midnight, reins in
to an easy canter, or a song begun
fades out, its melody unexplored.
How true the old adage: love's miracle poured

on the green years seldom bears fruit:
for a season only the leaves are ripe.
Too soon, death's white slow-dance:
only the lucky get a second chance.

THE GARDEN OF FORGETTING

There is a thirsty road that winds
around the mountain's waist and ends
in the Garden of Forgetting; there,
yesterday, today and tomorrow grows,

and the night-blooming cereus stays
awake until the day unfolds,
and time passes in a dream of light.

There the bottlebrush sweeps the earth,
its red prickle weeping
to the silence of terraced stone,
the sky with its tongues of flame.

But there is one tree (no one knows
its name) whose uncertain tendrils find
their way through snowy branches
of euphorbia; and now

yesterday, today and tomorrow weeps
in the Garden of Forgetting,
in fading light.

WAITING FOR THE TRAIN

The pneumatic doors shut
on a cold wind, warmed by the turning
pistons; a trench-coat juts
through the sealed crack, like yearning.

I wait in that lonely place
now emptied of the sea
of blank cellophane faces –
bound for what destiny?

My mind turns to his room –
the tumour spreads like night –
and I wonder how long or how soon
before time throws this fight.

The days are getting shorter,
winter is almost here,
and I recall a summer,
the sea gulls circling a clear

blue sky at low tide, peace-
ably swooping the water,
driftwood waving a piece
of cloth, white like surrender.

Where is the Lord God now?
When time's indifference wrenches
us from contentment, we bow
and break like thirsty branches.

Perhaps tonight the train
will come –for what destiny?
When time draws back the pain,
is its aim eternity?

THE CLOWN

When the spotlight fades, look at the clown's
painted-on smile, brimming with tears,
dissolving as the mask comes down.

Look at the woman sitting there,
like Smile's unfinished masterpiece:
An artist's retrospective of
the sorrow no one wants to hear.

Listen to the night applaud
as soundlessly the laughter dies
and flaccid reminiscence lies
insubstantial as a cloud

settling on the morning's dreamless sleep.
Look how the watchful night allows
its veil to mask tomorrow's eyes,
like us, our sorrow, while we weep.

GUYANA SEASON

She had not known the back streets of that country,
the brackished water of her history's creeks,
the mist-white roar of Kaieteur,
a bone in the throat of the ocean,
when he came, hiding his pain in pedantry,
raging in between the pages of history
till negritude grew from the iron's gouge
and the tears of generations fell at their feet.
She remembers the year like the swill of fine wine;
the sea grapes desiccated like goat trails
on the hot sand, the hermit crabs retreated
to cracks in the reef. When the wind fell silent
on the tremulous water, only sorrow remained,
and the *whoosh* of ripe almond leaves, washing the shore.

GUYANA GOLD

Looking back, the dark was always there, like the cedar door
that graced the fret-worked portico of a childhood home.
Now I remember its shelter, not the storm's outpour-
ing on startled faces, the day uncertainty marked time.

The memory of those years remains certain as the road
parting the sea where wind prickles its glass or a message
fired in cobalt as the celibate wrestles with God:
Some indiscretions reap inconsolable loss.

Yet nothing sought or learned prepared me for Black Gold,
its paradox, that country where rivers run backwards
from the south, hiding their dark in the spume-white cold
that pummels the sea where thirst yearns upwards.

We'd met in the early spring, renewal damp
in the expectant earth. He could have been my son
in another life. How could I have known, this camp
dougla with the sun in his eyes still wore indentured skin.

Listen, you can hear the weeping even as forgiveness spawns
like salmon in brackish gray. Time keeps its slaves.
One day, through drowsy sight as I watched a piper churn
the sea where ripe almond leaves shuffle in salt waves,

I suddenly saw the truth unveiled – not like the truth
that screws, loosening, bleed on a schooner's hull,
nor the moon erased from the crown of hills,
the sun between two peaks, but in what we cull

where the galaxies bear witness to new beginnings,
where hunger, insatiable, scratches the chasm of loss,
or, the gambler, emptying a lifetime's winnings
in wide saucers, finds the dream reversing chaos.

CRESCENT MOON

Through dawn's grey curtain a mint-green coat
disappears; a door is shut; a bus lurches toward
a narrow road, the light dwindling like a cat's
eyes closing in the dark. A sea rises in my throat.

I remember a tree's hollowed-out torso standing
like a totem in the middle of a field. Each day
the birds would sit in the naked branches, some listening
at the heartless cavern, or flying off in search

of food for their young, or twigs and straw;
perhaps, just knowing they could return –
not like their human counterpart, stitched in
some narrow line, afraid of venturing out, of dearth.

Is there a colder wind than the one that rattles
the rusting hinges of autumn's door, while Orion
dreams of spring? Each season brings its salt,
even as a tree's dry stump makes a resting-place for birds.

Now, we double back and forth along a path
oblivious to the snap of twigs under hurrying feet,
a road weeping in a mountain's war-torn earth,
or simply the joy of a flat line, a skipping stone.

As if learning nothing from the past (yet always
trailing its thin, pitying light over our heads,
behind our backs, the crescent moon), we carry on.

ABOUT THE AUTHOR

Gwyneth Barber Wood began writing as a young adult and has been making her way in poetry through workshops with Wayne Brown, poet and editor for *The Jamaica Observer*, Arts Section, where her poems appear regularly. In 1999 she placed third for poetry in *The Jamaica Observer Arts Section* Awards. The following year, she was awarded the bronze medal and merit certificate for two poems in the JCDC Literary Awards competition.

A two time fellow of the Virginia Centre for the Creative Arts (VCCA), spring 2001 and 2003, she was among the poets invited to read at the Calabash International Literary Festival in 2001 hosted by Jake's on the south coast of Jamaica.

Some of her poems are included in the 2000/2001/2002 anthologies *Bearing Witness* published by the *Jamaica Observer* and edited by Wayne Brown, and in the 2002 Spring issue of *Artemis Journal*, the online issue of poetrymagazine.com, March 2003 and *The Caribbean Writer*, an anthology published by the University of the Virgin Islands.

In May 2002 she was invited to read at Festival-in-the-Park in Roanoke, Virginia, and during that visit also gave a private reading, organized by Judy Light Ayyildiz, poet and author of memoir *Nothing but Time*, and co-hosted by the VCCA.

She recently attended the University of the West Indies, department of Literatures in English course 2003-2004 (History of the Sonnet) where a selection of her sonnets were part of the course material.

Gwyneth Barber Wood is married with one son and currently resides in Jamaica where she was born.

OTHER JAMAICAN POETRY TITLES FROM PEEPAL TREE

Opal Palmer Adisa, *Caribbean Passion*
1-900715-92-9 £7.99

Lloyd Brown, *Duppies*
0-948833-83-1, £6.95

Kwame Dawes, *Progeny of Air*
0-948833-68-8, £7.95

Kwame Dawes, *Prophets*
0-948833-85-8, £7.95

Kwame Dawes, *Jacko Jacobus*
0-948833-85-8, £7.95

Kwame Dawes, *Requiem*
0-948833-85-8, £5.99

Kwame Dawes, *Shook Foil*
1-900715-14-7, £7.99

Kwame Dawes, *New and Selected Poems*
1-900715-70-8, £9.99

Marcia Douglas, *Electricity Comes to Cocoa Bottom*
1-900715-28-7, £6.99

Gloria Escoffery, *Mother Jackson Murders the Moon*
1-900715-24-4, £6.99

John Figueroa, *The Chase*
0-948833-52-1 £8.95

Delores Gauntlett, *The Watertank Revisited*
0-84523-009-4

Jean Goulbourne, *Woman Song*
1-900715-57-0, £6.99

Rachel Manley, *A Light Left On*
0-948833-55-6, £5.99

Earl McKenzie, *Against Linearity*
0-948833-85-8, £7.95

Earl McKenzie, *The Almond Leaf* (forthcoming)
1-84523-012-4, £7.99

Anthony McNeill, *Chinese Lanterns from the Blue Child*
1-900715-18-X, £6.99

Geoffrey Philp, *Florida Bound*
0-948833-82-3, £5.95

Geoffrey Philp, *Hurricane Center*
1-900715-23-6, £6.99

Geoffrey Philp, *Xango Music*
1-900715-46-5, £6.99

Velma Pollard, *Crown Point*
0-948833-24-6, £7.99

Velma Pollard, *Shame Trees Don't Grow Here*
0-948833-48-3, £6.99

Velma Pollard, *Leaving Traces* (forthcoming)
1-84523-021-3, £7.99

Heather Royes, *Days and Nights of the Blue Iguana*
ISBN 1 84523 019 1

Ralph Thompson, *The Denting of a Wave*
0-948833-62-9, £6.95

Ralph Thompson, *Moving On*
1-900715-17-1, £7.99

Ralph Thompson, *View from Mount Diablo*
1-900715-81-3, £7.99

All available from Peepal Tree Press's website, with secure, on-line
ordering. Visit peepaltreepress.com
or contact us my mail at 17 King's Avenue, Leeds LS6 1QS, UK